PENNSYLVANIA

in words and pictures

BY DENNIS B. FRADIN

ILLUSTRATIONS BY RICHARD WAHL

MAPS BY LEN W. MEENTS

Consultant:
Lucille Wallower

 CHILDRENS PRESS ®

CHICAGO

For Jaynie Biaselle Wilcox, formerly of Philadelphia

Pennsylvania farm

Library of Congress Cataloging in Publication Data

Fradin, Dennis B.
  Pennsylvania in words and pictures.

  SUMMARY: A brief history of the Keystone State with
a description of its countryside and major cities.
  1. Pennsylvania—Juvenile literature. [1. Pennsyl-
vania] I. Wahl, Richard, 1939- II. Meents, Len W.
III. Title.
F149.3.F7   974.8   79-24942
ISBN 0-516-03938-5

Picture Acknowledgments:
PHILADELPHIA CONVENTION AND VISITORS BUREAU—cover, pages
27, 29
POCONO MOUNTAINS VACATION BUREAU—pages 2, 39
GETTYSBURG TRAVEL COUNCIL, INC.—pages 4, 21, 22, 30
OLD BEDFORD VILLAGE—pages 10, 11, 12
PENNSYLVANIA DUTCH VISITORS BUREAU—pages 13, 37
MONTGOMERY COUNTY CONVENTION AND VISITORS BUREAU—
pages 18, 19, 41
NATIONAL PARK SERVICE, JOHNSTOWN FLOOD NATIONAL
MEMORIAL—page 24
HARRISBURG-HERSHEY TOURIST PROMOTION AGENCY—page 25
HARRISBURG PARKS AND RECREATION DEPARTMENT—page 31
HERCO, INC. HERSHEY INFORMATION CENTER—page 32
GREATER PITTSBURGH CHAMBER OF COMMERCE—page 33
PITTSBURGH CONVENTION AND VISITORS BUREAU—page 34
ARCHITECT OF THE U.S. CAPITOL—page 35
COVER—Modern-day Benjamin Franklin at the Liberty Bell

Pennsylvania

Pennsylvania (pen • sill • VAIN • ee • ah) is one of our loveliest states. It has mountains and forests where deer and bears live. In big cities many things are made. Pennsylvania is the leading steel-producing state. It is also one of the leading coal-mining states. Pennsylvania has much more. . .

Do you know where the Declaration of Independence (deck • lair • RAY • shun uv in • dih • PEN • dence) was adopted?

Do you know where the United States Constitution (con • stih • TOO • shun) was signed?

Lincoln Speech Memorial in Gettysburg National Park

Do you know where Abraham Lincoln gave the Gettysburg (GET • ees • berg) Address after a big Civil War battle?

Do you know where the biggest chocolate factory in the world is?

As you will learn, the answer to all these questions is: Pennsylvania.

About 300 million years ago, Pennsylvania was covered by swamps. Plants lived in the swamps. The plants died. Over millions of years the plants were pressed into coal. That is why Pennsylvania has so much coal today.

If you push the ends of a rug together, it will rise in the middle. That is how the Appalachian (app • uh • LAY • chun) Mountains were folded out of the earth. It happened about 200 million years ago.

Long before there were people in Pennsylvania there were interesting animals. Dinosaurs (DINE • ah • sores) lived there. So did woolly mammoths. They looked like big hairy elephants.

People were living in Pennsylvania at least 10,000 years ago. They fished. They hunted. They were *nomads* who followed animal herds for food. These early people may have been related to the Indians who came later.

At one time, at least 15,000 Indians lived in Pennsylvania. Some of the Indian tribes in Pennsylvania were the Delaware (DELL • ah • ware), Shawnee (shaw • NEE), Seneca (SEN • ih • kah), and Susquehannock (suss • kwih • HAN • uck).

The first known outsiders in Pennsylvania were the Dutch. They were from the Netherlands (NEH • ther • landz). In 1609 Henry Hudson explored the region for the Dutch. The Dutch explorer Cornelius Hendricksen (kor • NEEL • yus HEN • drik • sen) explored the Philadelphia area in 1616. Dutchmen came to trade with the Indians. They gave pans, knives, guns, and tools to the Indians. In return the Indians gave them valuable furs.

Sweden (SWEE • din) also claimed the land. In 1643 Swedish settlers came to live on Tinicum Island (TIN • ih • come EYE • lund). That is near where Philadelphia stands today. Swedish people built the first permanent settlements in Pennsylvania. In 1664 the English (ING • lish) took control of the land.

A young man named William Penn lived in England.
He decided to become a Quaker (KWAY • ker). The
Quakers were also known as the Society of Friends.
They were a religious group. They believed that all
people were equal. They hated fighting. They dressed
simply—usually in black. Quakers in England were often
put in jail.

William Penn's father died. The king of England owed
him some money. That money was now owed to William
Penn.

Penn asked the king for land in America instead of the money. The king agreed. He named the land *Pennsylvania*—meaning *Penn's Woods*. William Penn got many of his Quaker friends out of jail.

In 1682 Penn sailed for America. Three boatloads of Quakers went with him. They had cows, chickens, and other things they would need in America. Many people died on the ships as they crossed the ocean. Finally, the ships arrived in America. The Quakers founded Chester. In 1682 they founded Philadelphia (which means *brotherly love*). William Penn made some laws for the Pennsylvania colony. They were called the *Frame of Government.* These laws gave the people a lot of freedom. But Pennsylvania was an English colony. The king of England was the ruler over all.

Other religious groups in Europe were treated badly. "Come to Pennsylvania," said William Penn. And they did. Many people of different kinds of beliefs settled there. By 1700 Philadelphia was a booming town of 4,000 people. Over the years, many German, Welsh, and Scots-Irish people made new homes in "Penn's Woods."

At first, the settlers and the Indians were friends. The Indians taught the settlers to grow corn and other crops. They showed them trails through the woods. William Penn was fair to the Indians.

William Penn's meeting with the Indians. Painting by Benjamin West.

At Old Bedford Village blacksmiths, broommakers, leatherwrights, furniture makers, and cabinet makers work in reconstructed colonial shops.

Some early settlers set up shops and stores in Philadelphia. In 1690 the first paper mill in America was set up in Philadelphia. Other craftsmen made glass. Some built ships. Still others began mining iron. Many settlers moved west of Philadelphia to farm.

Farm families often settled near rivers. The Indians had done this also. Crops grew well in the river valleys. The rivers provided drinking water for people and animals.

Colonial farm families often settled near rivers.
This is the Egolf farm at Old Bedford Village.

Farm families built log cabins and barns. They planted their crops with wooden farm tools. Deer, bears, small animals, and birds provided meat. Bear skins made good blankets. The fireplace was the center of the house. There the food was cooked. In the winter it kept the settlers warm.

Colonists built their log cabins close together for protection.

The kitchen fireplace was the center of the house.

Hex signs can still be seen on Pennsylvania Dutch barns.

The German people in Pennsylvania called themselves *Deutsch* (DOYTCH), which means German. Others called them *Pennsylvania Dutch*. Some of these people painted pretty designs (dih • ZINES) on their barns. The designs were thought to be hex signs to keep away witches. Today we think that these are just decorations.

The Pennsylvania Dutch became well known for making apple butter and other tasty dishes. They brought pretzels to America. They invented many things. They built the famous Conestoga (kahn • ess • TOE • gah) wagons. These were used to transport their goods to market. Later, these wagons took many settlers out West. The Pennsylvania Dutch also made the first "long rifles." These rifles were later used in Kentucky and elsewhere.

William Penn had been fair to the Indians. But he died in 1718. After that, the Indians were cheated out of much land. Many Indians had to move to the Susquehanna (suss • kwih • HAN • ah) Valley. That is in northeastern Pennsylvania. The Indians were angry.

The French also claimed much land in America. Some was in western Pennsylvania. In 1754 war broke out between the French and the English. Most Pennsylvania

Indians sided with the French. They didn't like the way the English had treated them. The war they fought is called the French and Indian War. In the first battles, the French and the Indians beat the English near Fort Duquesne (doo • KAIN), now Pittsburgh. A young soldier named George Washington fought for the English in these battles.

By 1763 the English had won the French and Indian War. They now controlled Pennsylvania and the rest of their 13 colonies.

England had to pay for the French and Indian War. The king of England made people in America pay heavy taxes. People had come to Pennsylvania and the other colonies to be free. They didn't want to pay these taxes. They were also beginning to think of themselves as Americans. They didn't want to be ruled by the king of England any more.

"Give me liberty or give me death!" said Patrick Henry of Virginia. Many other people talked of forming a new free country. It would be the United States of America. To do this, they would have to go to war with England. Many were not willing to do that.

Men from the 13 colonies met in Philadelphia. They would decide what to do. They called their group the

Continental Congress. The second time they met, Thomas Jefferson wrote the *Declaration of Independence.* It said that the United States was free of England.

On July 4, 1776, the Congress voted to adopt the Declaration of Independence. Today, Americans call that day the birthday of the United States.

On July 8, 1776, a bell was rung at the Philadelphia State House. This bell is now called the Liberty Bell. People met to hear the Declaration of Independence. They knew this meant war with England.

The Liberty Bell

Revolutionary War (rev • oh • LOO • shun • airy wore) battles were fought in Pennsylvania. George Washington led the American army. The English wanted to capture Philadelphia. On September 11, 1777, George Washington and about 11,000 men lost the Battle of Brandywine (BRAN • dee • wine), near Philadelphia. The next month, the English took Philadelphia. Washington and his men had to retreat.

The Peter Wentz Farmstead, used as a headquarters by George Washington

Huts and cannon in Valley Forge National Historical Park

Washington led his men to Valley Forge (FORJ), about 25 miles west of Philadelphia. There they spent the winter. The men were cold. They were hungry. But they did not give up hope. Americans wanted freedom. In the spring there were fresh troops. There were many more battles. The United States finally won the Revolutionary War in 1783.

In 1787 another important paper was written in Philadelphia. This was the law of our land: the United States Constitution.

On December 12, 1787, Pennsylvania became the second state. It was nicknamed the *Keystone* (KEE • stone) *State.* A keystone is a stone that holds other stones in place. In many ways Pennsylvania had helped hold the young country together. The capital of the United States is now Washington, D.C. But between 1790 and 1800 Philadelphia was the capital.

People farmed in Pennsylvania. They also began to manufacture (make) things there. They made iron. They made farm tools, stoves, and nails from the iron. In 1859 Edwin L. Drake drilled an oil well near Titusville. This began Pennsylvania's oil industry. Coal was also mined in Pennsylvania.

By the 1860s railroads crossed the state. Now products could be sent from Pennsylvania to the rest of America.

War between the Northern and Southern states broke out in 1861. This is called the Civil War. Southerners talked of *states' rights*. They felt that each state should decide for itself about slavery and other issues.

Pennsylvania was a Northern state. Most Pennsylvania people felt that all states should have the same laws. They did not like slavery. Some even helped slaves escape to Canada on the *underground railroad.* This was a series of hiding places. Slaves hid in these places on their flight to freedom.

The Keystone State sent about 340,000 soldiers to fight in the Northern army.

The Dobbin House was used as a "station" on the underground railroad

Photograph of Abraham Lincoln (arrow) giving
the Gettysburg Address on November 19, 1863.

There was one huge battle in Pennsylvania. On July 1, 1863, General George Meade went to Gettysburg. He and his Northern soldiers fought against General Robert E. Lee and his Southern soldiers. The Battle of Gettysburg was one of the bloodiest battles in United States history. Over 38,000 Americans were killed or wounded. Lee and his Southern troops lost. Three months after the fight, President Abraham Lincoln visited the battlefield. He gave his famous Gettysburg Address there. He wanted people to remember all those who had died in the war that divided North and South.

After the Civil War, industry boomed. More and more coal was mined. It was used to heat buildings. It was used to make steel. People from around the world came to live and work in the steel cities of Pennsylvania. Pittsburgh became the biggest steel-making city in the world. And Pennsylvania became the leading steel state. Pennsylvania was becoming mainly a manufacturing state—as it is today.

People came to Pennsylvania from far-off countries. They brought their own customs, foods, and stories.

People came to Pennsylvania to have a better life. But many who worked in the mines and steel mills earned very little money. In the late 1800s there were riots in Pennsylvania cities. Workers wanted higher pay.

During World War I (1914-1918) and World War II (1939-1945) Pennsylvania produced many weapons.

In 1977, a big flood hit Johnstown. That wasn't the first time. In 1936 Johnstown and Pittsburgh had been hard hit by floods. But the worst flood in Johnstown was in 1889. In the spring of that year the Conemaugh (KAHN • ih • maw) and Stony Creek rivers rose higher and higher. On May 31 the dam holding the waters back burst. A 75-foot-tall wall of water smashed the city. Buildings were carried away like toys. More than 2,200 people died in the great Johnstown Flood.

Destruction caused by the 1889 Johnstown Flood

Three Mile Island nuclear plant

The electricity in your house may come from a nuclear reactor. In 1979 there was an accident at the Three Mile Island nuclear reactor near Harrisburg. Harmful radiation leaked from the reactor. Many people in the area left their homes. Scientists and lawmakers saw that more care must be taken to prevent such accidents.

Today, Pennsylvania still has the beautiful scenery it had when only Indians lived there. It is the leading iron and steel-producing state. And it has many places to visit that are important to American history.

You have learned about some of Pennsylvania's history. Now it is time for a trip—in words and pictures—through the Keystone State.

Pennsylvania is a wonderland of green. About 60 percent of the state is still covered by forests. Appalachian Mountain ranges rise high above much of the state. The Allegheny Mountains are in this range.

There are many farms in Pennsylvania. Corn is a leading crop. Other farm products include mushrooms, potatoes, tobacco, apples, and peaches. Pennsylvania is also a leading milk state. Beef cattle and eggs come from some Pennsylvania farms.

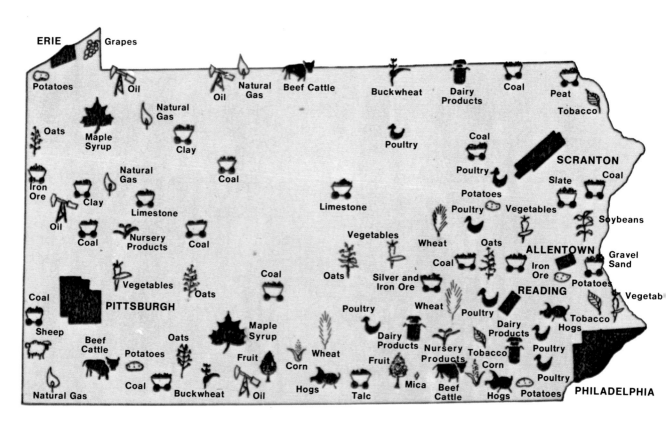

Above: Sailing on the Schuylkill
(SKOOL • kill) River
Left: Modern-day Benjamin Franklin
at Independence Hall

Philadelphia is a good place to begin your trip through Pennsylvania. It is the state's biggest city. It is the fourth biggest city in the United States. Delaware Indians once lived there. The town was founded in 1682 by William Penn and his Quaker Friends. Two of the city's nicknames are the *Quaker City* and the *City of Brotherly Love.* There is a statue of William Penn on top of Philadelphia's City Hall.

If you could go back in a time machine, you would meet some interesting people in Philadelphia: William Penn; Thomas Jefferson; and Benjamin Franklin, printer and inventor.

You can't see these people. But you can see the buildings where they lived and worked. Visit Independence Hall, in Independence National Historical (hiss • TORE • ih • kull) Park. There, the Declaration of Independence was adopted. The United States Constitution was adopted there, too. Behind Independence Hall you can see the Liberty Bell.

You probably have a United States flag in your classroom. We think that Betsy Ross made the *first* United States flag in about 1777. Visit her house on Arch Street. In Elfreth's Alley you can see houses that were built when Betsy Ross and Benjamin Franklin lived in Philadelphia.

Philadelphia has many places that are the oldest in the United States. The Library Company of Philadelphia was founded in 1731 by Benjamin Franklin. It was the first library in the United States to lend out books. The Pennsylvania Academy of the Fine Arts houses the oldest art museum in the United States.

Outdoor activities in Philadelphia include sailing and going to the zoo.

There is much to do outdoors. The Philadelphia Zoo is the oldest zoo in the United States. Pennsylvanians love sports. The Philadelphia Phillies play baseball in Veterans Stadium. The Eagles play football in Veterans Stadium. The Flyers blast hockey pucks into the nets at the Spectrum. And the Philadelphia 76ers play basketball at the Spectrum.

When you leave Philadelphia, head west. Valley Forge National Historical Park is about 25 miles west of Philadelphia. That is where George Washington and his freezing soldiers spent the winter of 1777-1778.

West of Valley Forge is Gettysburg National Military Park. Visit this Civil War battlefield. Picture how it must have looked when 165,000 Americans fought there.

Cyclorama (sye • klo • RAM • ah) of Pickett's Charge during the Battle of Gettysburg

Above: View of Harrisburg from the
    Susquehanna River
Left: The Rockville Bridge, near
    Harrisburg. It is one of the largest
    stone-arch bridges in the world.

The city of Harrisburg is about 100 miles west of
Philadelphia. Harrisburg is the capital of Pennsylvania.
Visit the state capitol building. There, men and women
make laws for the Keystone State.

Just a few miles outside Harrisburg lies the town of Hershey. (HER • shee). Do you like chocolate? The world's *biggest* chocolate factory is in Hershey. You can see how chocolate is made.

Take the Pennsylvania Turnpike west from Harrisburg. You'll go through the mountains. Some of the mountaintops look blue from a distance. There are villages in the valleys.

In Hershey the streetlights look like Hershey kisses.

Pittsburgh's Golden Triangle. Here the Monongahela River and the
Allegheny River join to form the Ohio River.

In southwestern Pennsylvania you will come to the
state's second biggest city. This is Pittsburgh. It lies
where the Monongahela (mah • non • gah • HEE • lah) and
Allegheny (AL • ih • gain • ee) rivers fork to form the Ohio
(oh • HI • oh) River. Do you see all those bridges?
Pittsburgh has more bridges—over 700—than any other
United States city. That is because of the three rivers in
the city.

Today, Pittsburgh is the leading steel-making city in
the world. Its nickname is the *Steel City.*

Visit Pittsburgh's Museum of Natural History. There you can see fossils of dinosaurs and Egyptian (ee • GYP • shun) mummies. If you want to learn about the stars, visit the Buhl Planetarium (BYOOL plan • ih • TAIR • ee • um). Pittsburgh also has a fine symphony (SIM • foe • nee) orchestra and art galleries.

At Three Rivers Stadium you can see the Pirates play baseball. You can also see Pittsburgh's pro football team play there. What do you think the football team in the *Steel City* is called? The Pittsburgh Steelers.

Three Rivers Stadium at night

The Battle of Lake Erie. Painting by William H. Powell.

If you go up the western side of Pennsylvania you will come to the state's third biggest city—Erie (EE • ree). The city lies on Lake Erie. Once, Erie and Seneca Indians lived in the area. The town of Erie was founded in 1795.

Boats go in and out of the port of Erie. Ships bring in iron ore. This iron is used to make steel in Erie and other Pennsylvania cities.

Visit Presque Isle (PRESK EYE • ull) State Park in Erie. During the War of 1812, the United States fought England on Lake Erie. Commodore Oliver Hazard Perry built a fleet of boats in Presque Isle Bay. Perry defeated the English with these boats. You can see his flagship, the *Niagara.*

Scranton (SKRAN • tun) is Pennsylvania's fifth biggest city. It is in northeastern Pennsylvania. It lies in a valley of the Appalachian Mountains. This is a big coal-mining area.

Allentown (AL • en • town) is Pennsylvania's fourth biggest city. Trucks, buses, and machines are made there. Many Pennsylvania Dutch people live in Allentown.

Nearby Bethlehem (BETH • leh • hem) has a huge steel mill. It produces steel for products made in Allentown. Bethlehem was founded by the Moravians in 1741. They are a Pennsylvania Dutch religious group.

Philadelphia, Pittsburgh, Erie, Allentown, and Scranton are the five biggest cities in Pennsylvania. But the big cities tell only part of the state's story. During your travels through Pennsylvania you'll see small towns.

Many Pennsylvania Dutch still live in the state. Most of them live in the east. Many still follow their old customs.

The Amish (AH • mish) are a religious group of the Pennsylvania Dutch. They are one of the religious groups called the "plain people." The women wear long dresses and bonnets. The men have long beards. They wear black suits and wide-brimmed hats. The Amish travel in horse-drawn wagons. They do not drive cars. They farm with horses and plows. They do not use modern farm machines. Visit the Amish Homestead, near Lancaster (LANG • kass • ter). At this farm you can learn about these peaceful people.

Three Amish boys

Hopewell Village is a National Historic Site. It is south of Birdsboro (BERDZ • burro). This was an early iron-making town. There you can see where cannon and ammunition were made during the Revolutionary War.

Traveling through Pennsylvania, you will also see many coal-mining towns. Some of them are Hazleton (HAYZ • ill • tun), Uniontown (YOON • yun • town), Coaldale (KOLE • dayle), Lansford (LANZ • ferd), and Black Lick.

On your trip through Pennsylvania, you will also see many places of natural beauty. Pine Creek Gorge is near Wellsboro. It is a canyon. It was carved out long ago by the Pine Creek River.

People enjoy skiing, hiking, and canoing in Pennsylvania's mountains. The Pocono (POH • kuh • no) Mountains are lovely. They have sparkling waterfalls.

Bushkill Falls, deer, and
canoeing in the Pocono Mountains.

One is Bushkill Falls. The Delaware Water Gap is a
pretty gorge in the Pocono Mountains.

People are not the only ones who enjoy Pennsylvania's
forests and mountains. Many deer and black bears still
live in the state. Pennsylvania has a place where hawks,
eagles, and other birds can live safely. It is called the
Hawk Mountain Bird Sanctuary.

Places can't tell the whole story of Pennsylvania. Many interesting people have lived in the Keystone State.

Daniel Boone (1734-1820) was born in a log cabin near Reading (RED • ing), Pennsylvania. He became a famous trailblazer and frontiersman.

Benjamin Franklin (1706-1790) was born in Boston. When he was seventeen years old he ran away to Philadelphia. Franklin became a printer. He published *The Pennsylvania Gazette* and *Poor Richard's Almanac.* He founded the school that grew into the University of Pennsylvania. He founded a hospital and a library. He was also a scientist, inventor, and famous statesman. He signed both the Declaration of Independence and the United States Constitution.

James Buchanan (byoo • CAN • an) was born near Mercersburg (MER • serz • berg). He became a lawyer. In 1865 he was elected the 15th President of the United States.

Mary Cassatt (kah • SAHT) was born in Pittsburgh in 1845. She studied painting at the Pennsylvania Academy of the Fine Arts. She became a great American painter.

Marian Anderson was born in Philadelphia in 1902. She was a poor black girl. But she had a gift. She became a famous concert singer. In 1955, Marian Anderson became the first black person to sing with New York's Metropolitan Opera.

John James Audubon (AW • duh • bahn) came to live near Philadelphia when he was eighteen. He was an artist. He loved to paint pictures of birds. His book of paintings, *Birds of America,* became very famous.

Left: John James Audubon
Below: Mill Grove, Audubon's home

In more recent times, Pennsylvania has produced some interesting people. Baseball player Reggie Jackson was born in Wyncote (WIN • coat) in 1946. He became famous for hitting five home runs in the 1977 World Series. Other famous baseball players from Pennsylvania include Roy Campanella (kam • pen • ELL • ah), Stan Musial (MYOO • zial), and Honus Wagner (HOE • nuss WAG • ner). Football star Joe Namath was born in Beaver Falls. An astronaut, Charles Conrad, Jr., was born in Philadelphia. He was part of the Apollo 12 mission that landed on the moon.

Home to the Delaware Indians . . . William Penn . . . and Benjamin Franklin.

The place where the Declaration of Independence and the Constitution were adopted.

A state that produces steel . . . coal . . . and chocolate.

This is Pennsylvania—the Keystone State.

Facts About PENNSYLVANIA

Area—45,333 square miles (33rd biggest state)

Borders—New York and Lake Erie on the north; New York and New Jersey across the Delaware River on the east; Delaware, Maryland, and West Virginia on the south; West Virginia and Ohio on the west

Greatest Distance North to South—169 miles

Greatest Distance East to West—307 miles

Highest Point—3,213 feet above sea level (Mount Davis)

Lowest Point—Sea level (along the Delaware River)

Hottest Recorded Temperature—111°F. (at Phoenixville, on both July 9 and 10, 1936)

Coldest Recorded Temperature—Minus 42°F. (at Smethport, on January 5, 1904)

Statehood—2nd state, on December 12, 1787 (Pennsylvania is officially called a *commonwealth)*

Capital—Harrisburg

Previous Capitals—Chester, Philadelphia, and Lancaster

Counties—67

U.S. Senators—2

U.S. Representatives—23

Electoral Votes—25

State Senators—50

State Representatives—203

State Motto—*Virtue, Liberty, and Independence*

Nickname—Keystone State

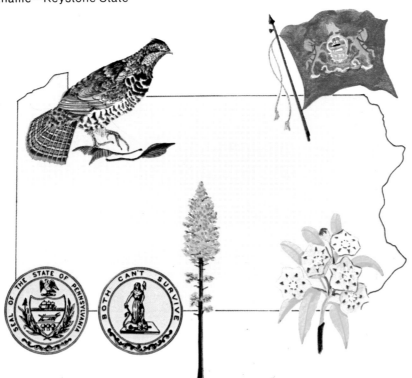

Origin of Name Pennsylvania—To honor Admiral Sir William Penn, father of
William Penn; it means "Penn's Woods"

State Seal—Adopted in 1893

State Flag—Adopted in 1907

State Coat of Arms—Used as long ago as 1777

Present Constitution Adopted—1968

State Flower—Mountain laurel

State Tree—Hemlock

State Bird—Ruffed grouse

State Insect—Firefly

State Dog—Great dane

State Animal—Whitetail deer

State Fish—Brook trout

State Colors—Blue and gold

Principal Rivers—Delaware, Susquehanna, Juniata, Lehigh, Schuylkill,
Allegheny, Monongahela, Ohio, Youghiogheny, Beaver, Clarion

Some Waterfalls—Bushkill, Winona, Raymondskill, Beaver, Buttermilk, Silver
Thread

Farm Products—Milk, beef cattle, sheep, poultry, eggs, corn, mushrooms,
apples, peaches, potatoes, winter wheat, hay, tobacco

Manufacturing—Steel, pig iron, many metal products, chocolate, potato chips,
pretzels, ice cream, other food products, glass products, electric equipment,
clothing, chemicals

Mining—Coal, limestone, iron ore, natural gas, oil

Population—1980 census: 11,879,679 (1993 estimate: 12,045,800)

Population Density—262 people per square mile

Population Distribution—69 per cent urban; 31 per cent rural

Major Cities	1980 Census	1990 Estimate
Philadelphia	1,684,740	1,557,637
Pittsburgh	423,959	400,681
Erie	119,123	111,713
Allentown	103,758	102,220
Scranton	88,117	82,299

Person per sq. mi.	Persons per km2
More than 300	More than 120
100 to 300	40 to 120
50 to 100	20 to 40
Less than 50	Less than 20

SCRANTON

PITTSBURGH

HARRISBURG

PHILADELPHIA

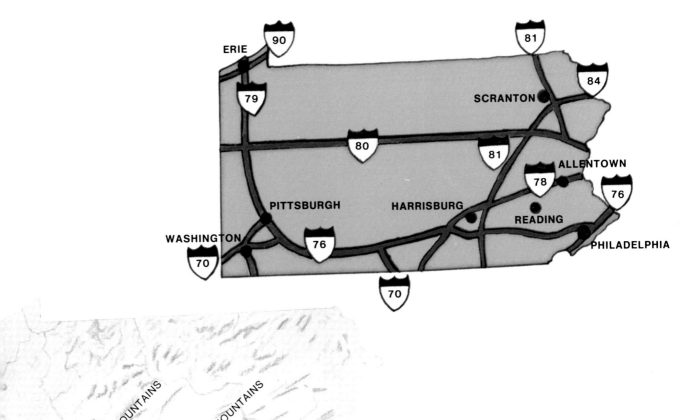

Pennsylvania History

There were people in Pennsylvania at least 10,000 years ago
1608—English Captain John Smith possibly enters Pennsylvania
1609—Henry Hudson, working for the Dutch, enters Delaware Bay
1616—Dutchman Captain Cornelius Hendricksen explores Philadelphia area;
      Frenchman Etienne Brulé explores Pennsylvania at about the same time
1643—Swedish people under Johan Printz settle at Tinicum Island
1644—William Penn is born on October 24
1664—English take control of Pennsylvania
1681—King Charles II of England grants "Penn's Woods" to William Penn
1682—William Penn arrives with other settlers; Philadelphia is begun
1690—First paper mill in America is built in Philadelphia
1701—Penn writes new constitution, called Charter of Privileges
1716—First iron forge in Pennsylvania is built near Pottstown
1718—William Penn, the father of Pennsylvania, dies on July 30

45

1723—Young Benjamin Franklin arrives in Philadelphia

1732—Steel is first made in Pennsylvania

1754—French and Indian War begins with fighting at Fort Duquesne near modern Pittsburgh

1763—English win French and Indian War and are in control of Pennsylvania

1774—First Continental Congress meets in Philadelphia

1775—Second Continental Congress meets in Philadelphia

1776—Declaration of Independence is adopted at Independence Hall on July 4

1777—Washington and his troops are defeated at Brandywine on September 11; in December they go to spend the winter at Valley Forge

1783—United States wins Revolutionary War!

1787—Constitution of United States signed in Philadelphia on September 17; on December 12 Pennsylvania becomes the 2nd state

1790—Philadelphia becomes the capital of the United States

1792—United States Mint is established in Philadelphia

1800—Washington, D.C. is now the nation's capital

1812—Harrisburg becomes capital of Keystone State

1813—Oliver Hazard Perry builds fleet of boats on Lake Erie during War of 1812

1859—Oil is found near Titusville

1860—2,906,215 people live in Keystone State

1861-1865—Civil War; over 340,000 Pennsylvanians fight on side of North

1863—Battle of Gettysburg fought from July 1-3; Lincoln gives Gettysburg Address on November 19

1876—Happy 100th birthday, United States! New invention—the telephone—is demonstrated at Philadelphia's Centennial Exhibition

1881—American Federation of Labor is formed at Pittsburgh

1887—Happy 100th birthday, Keystone State!

1889—Johnstown Flood kills at least 2,200

1897—Fire destroys State Capitol building in Harrisburg

1900—Population is 6,302,115

1906—New State Capitol building is completed

1914-1918—World War I; over 660,000 Pennsylvanians fight

1920—One of country's first radio stations, KDKA, is founded at Pittsburgh

1936—Big floods in Pennsylvania

1939-1945—World War II; 1,200,000 Pennsylvania men and women serve

1956—Pennsylvania Turnpike crosses state

1957—Nuclear reactor for generating electricity opens at Shippingport

1971—Pennsylvania begins individual income tax

1972—Hurricane Agnes causes much damage

1977—Floods hit Johnstown

1979—Nuclear accident at Three Mile Island nuclear plant near Harrisburg

1985—Philadelphia police firebomb home of MOVE, an organization of armed blacks, and fire spreads to neighboring homes; 11 dead, 200 homeless

1987—Robert P. Casey becomes governor

1988—Reverend Barbara C. Harris, a black Episcopal priest, is elected first woman Episcopal bishop; Tim Weiner of the *Philadelphia Inquirer* wins a Pulitzer Prize for journalism

INDEX

About the Author:

Dennis Fradin attended Northwestern University on a creative writing scholarship and was graduated in 1967. While still at Northwestern, he published his first stories in *Ingenue* magazine and also won a prize in *Seventeen's* short story competition. A prolific writer, Dennis Fradin has been regularly publishing stories in such diverse places as *The Saturday Evening Post, Scholastic, National Humane Review, Midwest,* and *The Teaching Paper.* He has also scripted several educational films. Since 1970 he has taught second grade reading in a Chicago school—a rewarding job, which, the author says, "provides a captive audience on whom I test my children's stories." Married and the father of three children, Dennis Fradin spends his free time with his family or playing a myriad of sports and games with his childhood chums.

About the Artists:

Len Meents studied painting and drawing at Southern Illinois University and after graduation in 1969 he moved to Chicago. Mr. Meents works full time as a painter and illustrator. He and his wife and child currently make their home in LaGrange, Illinois.

Richard Wahl, graduate of the Art Center College of Design in Los Angeles, has illustrated a number of magazine articles and booklets. He is a skilled artist and photographer who advocates realistic interpretations of his subjects. He lives with his wife and two sons in Libertyville, Illinois.